Contents

Notes about this Teaching Guide	4
The Football	9
No Presents for Christmas	13
Magpie Madness	17
Blubber and Floss	21
Jimmy and the Bluebottles	25
The Crossover	29
The Copperhead	33
Ratbags	37
Shape Shifters	41
Macca Dacca	45

Notes about this Teaching Guide

Introducing the Global Literacy Aussie Tales series

Students will love the *Aussie Tales* books. This new series is an exciting, high-quality resource, designed to encourage and motivate students to read while exploring Australian characters, values and cultural heritage.

The story lines, although fictional, are set in real places and relate the experiences of Australian characters. The readers will meet proactive characters involved in a variety of situations, from the everyday to the fantastic. The stories tackle a range of different issues and conclude with satisfactory outcomes. Black and white illustrations enhance each story.

Aussie Tales books cannot help but build confidence and encourage even reluctant readers to reach for every book in the series.

Books in the *Aussie Tales* series are suitable for students who are reading fluently. This series develops the reader's ability to deal with longer sentences and more complex vocabulary. As well, literary vocabulary is gradually introduced throughout the series. More challenging words used in the series have common root words or familiar prefixes and suffixes, allowing the reader to use a range of word analysis strategies without losing meaning. Both shorter and longer sentences are used to maintain an interesting flow of language. Complex paragraph structures are introduced and each illustration has been appropriately placed to aid comprehension and support the reader as they tackle the increasing level of difficulty in the language. Character descriptions develop throughout the series revealing the characters' thoughts, feelings and personalities in more depth.

Title	Reading age
The Football	7.5
No Presents for Christmas	7.75
Magpie Madness	8
Blubber and Floss	8.25
Jimmy and the Bluebottles	8.25
The Crossover	8.5
The Copperhead	8.75
Ratbags	8.75
Shape Shifters	9
Macca Dacca	9

Teaching Guide

By Jan Weeks

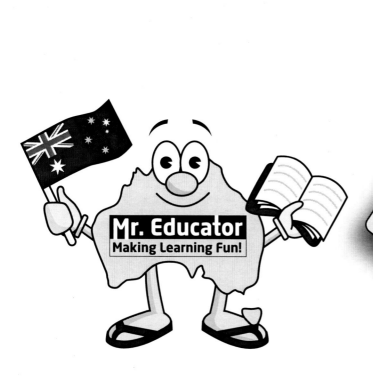

Global Literacy **Teaching Guide (Set 1)**
ISBN: 978-184285-155-5
Written by Jan Weeks
Copyright © Aussie School Books Pty Ltd and Jan Weeks 2009
Published in Europe, the Middle East and South Africa by Mr Educator in agreement with Aussie School Books Pty Ltd
P.O. Box 225
Abergele
Conway County LL18 9AY
North Wales
U.K.

DESIGNED

www.design-ed.com.au

Reproduction and Communication for other purposes

Except as permitted under the Act (for example a fair dealing for the purposes of study, research, criticism or review) no part of this book may be reproduced, stored in a retrieval system, communicated or transmitted in any form or by any means without prior written permission. All enquiries should be made to the publisher at the address above.

Copying of the blackline master pages

The purchasing educational institution and its staff are permitted to make copies of the pages marked as blackline master pages, beyond their rights under the Act, provided that:
1. the number of copies does not exceed the number reasonably required by the educational institution to satisfy its teaching purposes;
2. copies are made only by reprographic means (photocopying), not by electronic/digital means, and not stored or transmitted;
3. copies are not sold or lent; and
4. every copy made clearly shows the footnote ('Mr Educator. May be copied for non-commercial use in purchasing school only.').

For those pages not marked as blackline masters pages the normal copying limits in the Act, as described above, apply.

Aussie Tales and literacy

Being literate is vital to a happy and successful school life. Good reading skills help to achieve strong learning outcomes that spread across all facets of the school curriculum. As students learn to read in different ways, it is essential that emphasis be given to the development of these skills through a wide variety of activities.

The aim of independent reading should be to encourage students to think critically and be able to analyse and evaluate what they read. At this level, they should be able to:

- recognise mood and empathise with characters
- predict future occurrences
- improvise text, altering content to change story line
- call on previous knowledge and be able to form opinions
- make reference to authors and illustrators and be able to identify different parts of a book
- read independently for a sustained period of time and be able to recognise and discuss the grammatical features that constitute that text type
- access and record information for specific purposes.

Aussie Tales Teaching Guide

The Teaching Guide provides practical guidelines for classroom activities related to the books in the series. Together with the books themselves, the Teaching Guide aims to provide activities that will encourage students to:

- value reading as an important resource in our everyday lives
- see reading as an enjoyable activity that can be approached confidently and with the expectation of success
- use a range of skills and strategies to read and interpret written text
- recognise and understand the meaning of various punctuation marks
- identify tense and whether the text is written in first, second or third person
- develop an ever expanding vocabulary enhanced by the use of a dictionary
- identify setting, main characters, theme and occurrences in literary text and be able to identify the elements of structure such as orientation, complication and resolution.

In this Teaching Guide you will find:

- **Story facts**
  A summary of key facts is provided for each book.

- **Synopsis**
  A synopsis is provided for each book that gives teachers a quick summary of the story. It will assist teachers in introducing the book in an appropriate manner and may be useful as a guide to further resources.

- **Other activities**
  A number of suggestions for activities related to the themes of each title are provided. These include topics for general discussion and personal development, oral activities to promote understanding of how language works, research topics and ideas for creative expression.

- **Black line masters**
  There are three general black line masters (BLMs) for use with all the *Aussie Tales* books. Three specific BLMs are provided per book. These BLMs aid comprehension and encourage analytic and critical thinking as well as focusing on vocabulary, syntactic and comprehension skills.

Reading Log

Date	Title	Pages read

Awesome Words

As you read your *Aussie Tales* novels, write down some of the new or interesting words you find. Use a dictionary to find out the meaning.

Word	Meaning

Bookmark

Cut out these bookmarks and paste them back-to-back.
Colour and decorate as you wish.

Look for these values in the characters in your *Aussie Tales* books.

Care and Compassion
Characters caring for and being kind to others.

Doing Your Best
Characters trying hard to do the best job they can.

Fair Go
Characters making sure other people are treated fairly.

Freedom
Characters standing up for the rights of others.

Honesty and Trustworthiness
Characters being honest and truthful.

Integrity
Characters being honest and strong about what they believe is right.

Respect
Characters respecting other people's rights and points of view.

Responsibility
Characters being responsible for themselves, working out problems, taking care of the environment and doing things for their community.

Understanding, Tolerance and Inclusion
Characters being accepting of people who are different from them.

The Football

Story facts

Author:	Jeannie Meekins
Illustrator:	Tom Kurema
Text type:	Narrative
Person:	Third
Tense:	Past
Reading level:	24–26

Synopsis

Charlie would like to own the special Sherrin football signed by Nathan Buckley that he sees in a shop window but he doesn't have the money to buy it. His mother promises to buy him a football for his birthday but Charlie thinks that is too long to wait. His friend Liam suggests they pool their money and share the football but there is still not enough. They decide to do odd jobs to earn the money they need. At Mr Taylor's house, they discover their friend Simon's pet rabbit has died. Instead of buying the football, the boys decide to buy Simon another rabbit. Mr Taylor is so touched by their kindness that he rewards the boys with the football they intended to buy.

Other activities

✵ What type of game is Australian Rules and how is it played? Draw a chart to show the differences between Aussie Rules and Rugby League.

✵ In pairs, discuss the statement 'Pocket money should be earned.' Then write a report indicating your own opinion and giving reasons in support of your argument.

✵ Design a flyer advertising all the odd jobs you can do.

✵ List ten jobs you could do around your house or your neighbourhood to make money.

✵ Give a two-minute speech to describe your favourite sport or favourite sports star.

The Football

Syllables

Words are made up of chunks of sounds called syllables. Skim through the book and find five words to write in each column.

2-syllable	3-syllable	4-syllable

The Football

Who said it?

Write the names of the people in the story who said the following.

Come on, Charlie. We have to go home.   _____

We're trying to earn money to buy a football. Do you
have any jobs that need doing?   _____

Mrs Taylor wanted the garage cleaned out. Do you think
you boys could do that?   _____

Ten dollars! That's nearly half the money.   _____

Wayne usually does the grass.   _____

You've both done a really good job. Ten dollars each, just
as I told you.   _____

We'll get the rabbit. But next time we get the ball.   _____

Mum, look what Charlie and Liam gave me. Isn't he
beautiful?   _____

You know better than that. Put your bag in your room.   _____

We didn't buy the rabbit to get something back.   _____

Nouns, verbs and adjectives

Read the paragraph below. Underline all the nouns, draw a circle around all the verbs and draw a box around all the adjectives.

On Monday, when Charlie was walking home from school with his mum, he stopped at the sports shop window and looked in. The Nathan Buckley football was gone. There was an empty space where it had been. Charlie's stomach dropped. He checked all around the window in case it had been moved. But he couldn't see it anywhere.

The Football

What do you think?

Answer the following questions using complete sentences.

What did people do or use before there was money?
_____
_____

Why is it important for people to be able to write their signature?
_____
_____

Why do you think shopkeepers aren't allowed to employ children?
_____
_____

If you had to earn your own money, what kind of jobs would you like to do?
_____
_____

Why did the boys decide to buy the rabbit for Simon? Would you have done the same thing?
_____
_____

Football—a theme poem

Write a theme poem about football.

Theme poems have four lines.
Line 1 has 4 words
Line 2 has 3 words } rhyme
Line 3 has 4 words
Line 4 has 3 words } rhyme
Commas separate the words.

No Presents for Christmas

Story facts

Author	Barry Carozzi
Illustrator:	Steven Hallam
Text Type:	Recount
Person:	First
Tense:	Past
Reading level:	24–26

Synopsis

The story is set during the Great Depression. Times are hard in John's house. There is little money to feed and buy clothes for five children and five adults. Although the family is poor they are happy, but the thought of the coming Christmas with no presents makes them all a little sad. John and his sister Maggie meet a boy who has a mouth organ that he found at the tip. The children decide to look for presents for the family at the tip. They find gifts for everyone except their mother. On Christmas morning, John apologises to his mother for not getting her a present. She tells him that seeing the happy expressions on her family's faces when they received their gifts was the best present she could have.

Other activities

* Imagine you are used to getting presents for a special occasion each year. One year, there are no presents. Write a diary entry describing how you feel about receiving no presents.

* In pairs, have the students debate the topic 'It is better to give presents than receive them.'

* Choose three friends or family members and think of a present for each of them that doesn't cost any money. Write down a description of the presents and how you would make/find them.

* Read the job column in the newspaper. Cut out a job you'd like to do. Write an explanation of why that job appeals to you.

* Using the library and the Internet, research the Great Depression. Write down ten facts.

* Find out what happens to your garbage after it's collected. Draw a diagram to explain the process.

No Presents for Christmas

Homonyms: there, their, they're

There, their and *they're* are homonyms. Choose the correct word to fill in the gaps in the sentences.

Mother said to put the presents over _____.

The children found _____ gifts at the tip.

I think _____ going to have a good Christmas.

It was so difficult for _____ dad to get a job.

I wish _____ was something I could do to help.

_____ grandfather was often quite ill.

Was _____ grandmother born in England?

_____ not allowed go to the tip anymore.

Will _____ be turkey for Christmas dinner?

My uncle said _____ going away tomorrow.

> A homonym is a word having the same sound as another but different spelling and meaning, e.g. *bear, bare*.

No Presents for Christmas

Tense: present, past and future

Circle the tense used in each sentence.

I see the children going to the tip.	present	past	future
He gave me the book last week.	present	past	future
The girl is putting a bow in her hair.	present	past	future
Next week it will be raining.	present	past	future
John is asking Maggie to help him.	present	past	future
She saw the men looking for jobs.	present	past	future
They have eaten all their dinner.	present	past	future
I can hear Peter singing in the bath.	present	past	future
The children all received something.	present	past	future
Will you be going to school tomorrow?	present	past	future

No Presents for Christmas

Just the facts

Answer these questions about the story.

Name the people living in the house.
___
___

Where did the grandparents sleep?
___

Where did the children play?
___

Where did Dad go to look for a job?
___

What did Grandma use to make curtains?
___

At the beginning of the story, what pet did Pat have?
___

Where did the boy find his mouth organ?
___

Where was Grandma born?
___

What did they listen to on the radio on Christmas Eve?
___

What did Uncle Bill give the family to share on Christmas morning?
___

What did Dad say when he saw his new bike wheel?
___

Why was Mum crying on Christmas morning?
___
___

Magpie Madness

Story facts

Author:	Judi Pope
Illustrator:	Amy Geddes
Text Type:	Narrative
Person:	Third
Tense:	Past
Readling level:	26–28

Synopsis

Sam and her friend Diana are attacked by a magpie while riding their bikes to Sam's house. The local postie has also been attacked by a magpie and refuses to deliver mail to the houses in Sam's street until something is done to prevent the attacks. Sam decides to think up a way to stop the magpie attacks and enlists Diana's help.

The next day, a new girl called Bianca joins their class. At first, Bianca is rude to Diana about having cerebral palsy. Sam is angry on Diana's behalf but, when the teacher asks Sam and Diana to look after Bianca at break time, she is forced to agree. Sam and Diana discover that Bianca is living with her aunt for a while because her mother is too ill to take care of her. Bianca apologises to Diana for her earlier behaviour. Diana is happy to make friends but Sam is secretly still annoyed at Bianca.

Bianca learns of the girls' plans to stop the magpie attacks and has an idea that the girls try out. Unfortunately, their experiment ends with Bianca falling off her bike and getting concussion. While Diana goes for help, Sam thinks about how she has been holding a grudge against Bianca. She promises herself that she will be a good friend in future.

Sam also realises that they should try to make friends with the magpie rather than scaring it away. With the help of some juicy worms, the girls train the magpie not to attack.

Other activities

* In small groups, discuss whether it is ever all right for people in service industries, such as postal workers, to refuse to do their job.

* Design a sign warning people about swooping magpies.

* Make a list of rules worth remembering when riding a bike.

* In small groups, role-play the scene in the story when the teacher introduces Bianca to the class and Bianca doesn't want to sit next to Diana.

* In the story, Bianca comes from Canberra. Using the library or the Internet, find some information about Canberra and write down ten facts.

* In the story, Diana has a special bike. Research cerebral palsy and try to find some other special tools that are used by people with this condition.

Magpie Madness
Word usage

Synonyms

In the following sentences, replace each word in italics with a synonym.

Sam said, 'I *dislike* _____ magpies because they attack me.'

I *like* _____ magpies because they are *smart* _____.

The girls wore *identical* _____ uniforms to school.

Residents were *forced* _____ to *collect* _____ their mail from the post office.

Sam was *pleased* _____ that her *pal* _____ wasn't harmed.

A *big* _____, *fat* _____ magpie *sat* _____ on the fence.

The magpie *came* _____ to the *rear* _____ of Diana's *home* _____.

Sam's *mum* _____ was *concerned* _____ about Jim, the postal worker.

A synonym is a word that has the same meaning as another word. For example, sandals and flip-flops are synonyms.

Antonyms

In the following sentences, replace each word in italics with an antonym.

You *can* _____ ride your bike to school.

The girl *admired* _____ her teacher.

Earlier _____ in the week, a *man* _____ was attacked.

It's *wrong* _____ to be *unkind* _____ to my friends at school.

It'll be *difficult* _____ for Bianca to keep *new* _____ friends.

Peter *lost* _____ his hat *inside* _____ the tent.

Cats play *outside* _____ my house during the *day* _____.

The paper *boy* _____ had *many* _____ papers.

An antonym is a word that means the opposite of another word. For example, short and tall are antonyms.

Magpie Madness
Vocabulary building

Write down the dictionary definition of each word, then use it in a sentence to show you understand its meaning.

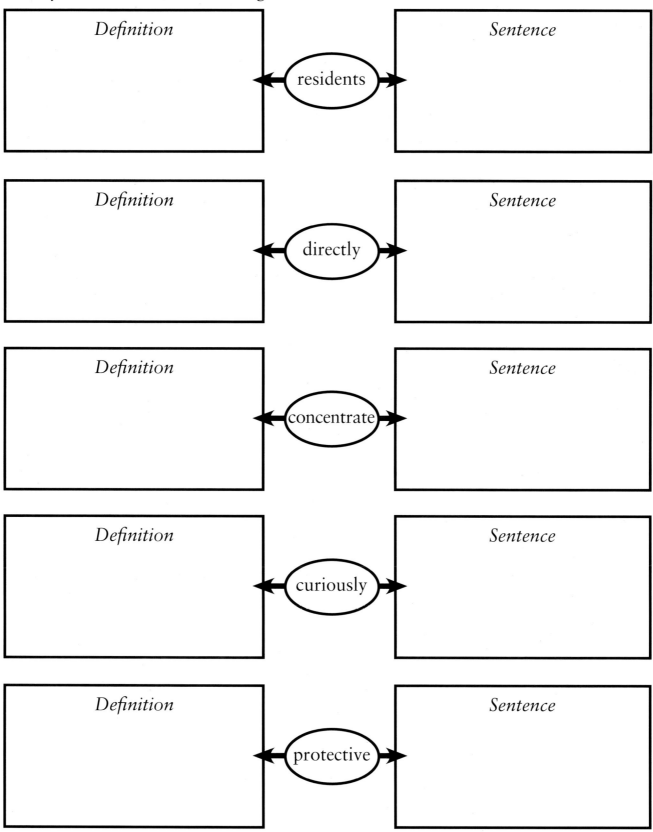

Magpie Madness

Complete the sentences

Use a word from the box to complete the sentences.

| injuries stay peck asked morning protect even |

It was very early in the _____ when Sam rode her bike.

Her mother always _____ her to wear a helmet.

A helmet would _____ Sam from the magpies.

Magpies like to _____ people with their beaks.

The pecks often cause _____ that can be very painful.

Sometimes they can _____ put people in hospital.

It was a good idea to _____ away from them.

Answer the following questions

1. Why did Sam dislike magpies?
   _____

2. What would you do to get rid of a magpie that was attacking you?
   _____
   _____

3. Why wasn't Bianca happy to go to Melbourne to stay with her aunt?
   _____
   _____

4. What would you have said to Bianca if she was being unkind to your friend who had cerebral palsy?
   _____
   _____

5. What might have happened if the girls hadn't tamed the magpie?
   _____
   _____

Blubber and Floss

Story facts

Author:	Liz Flaherty
Illustrator:	Rebecca Timmis
Text Type:	Narrative
Person:	Third
Tense:	Past
Reading level:	26–28

Synopsis

Sam is staying in a caravan at the beach with his parents and his sister, Max. They are on holidays with Sam's friend Ashley and her mother.

One day, while the children are at the local carnival, they hear a disturbance at the beach. A crowd has gathered to watch an elephant seal that is swimming nearby. Sam is thrilled and over the next few days the children make friends with the elephant seal, whom they name Henry. Henry is cheeky and enjoys playing tricks. Sometimes the tricks get him into trouble, such as when he upturns a small fishing boat while the owner is still in it. When the carnival is vandalised, the children suspect Henry is the culprit.

Ashley and Sam sneak out at night to find out what Henry gets up to. They fall asleep on the beach and when they wake up they discover that Henry has made his way to the carnival grounds and is sitting in one of the dodgem cars. The noise has alerted the carnival workers, who advance on Henry with cricket bats. Sam rushes in to protect Henry and Ashley uses the fairy floss machine to spray sticky fairy floss liquid at the angry carnival workers. While the carnies slip and slide all over the rink, Sam, Ashley and Henry make their escape. The next day, they find out that the carnival workers have packed up the carnival and moved on. The children plan to spend the rest of the holiday playing with Henry.

Other activities

* Imagine what it would be like to be a carnival worker. Write a diary entry for one day in your life, describing what you do.
* Write a newspaper article about a whale that is stranded on a beach.
* In small groups, discuss whether it was a good idea for the children to sneak out to the caravan at night.
* This story was inspired by a real-life elephant seal. Use the Internet to find some true stories about seals.
* Design your own carnival/fun park. Draw a plan, showing the layout.
* Research elephant seals and write down ten facts.

Blubber and Floss

BLM 1

Tense

Write future, present and past tense for the following words.

Present	Past	Future
e.g. comes	e.g. came	e.g. will come
	had	
		will leave
eats		
	brought	
		will make
catches		
	fell	
		will go
sees		

Punctuation marks

Select the correct punctuation mark to finish each sentence. Choose from full stops, question marks and exclamation marks.

Why were the carnies upset with Henry

What is that elephant seal doing now

Go away, you poor excuse for a fish

The children liked going on holidays

Who said you could wreck the carnival

Mum said elephant seals were wild animals

Nobody likes people who hurt animals

The carnival people packed up their tents

Okay, okay, if you have to

Stop chasing my elephant seal

Blubber and Floss

Sequencing

Number the sentences in the order in which they occur in the story.

☐ The fisherman plunged into the water, waving a meaty fist at Henry.
☐ The brown blob splashed and tumbled in the choppy water.
☐ The rubbery floor was awash with oodles of cobwebby fairy floss.
☐ Suddenly, his board shot up from underneath him and he rocketed into the air.
☐ Ashley peered along the moonlit beach, searching for the elephant seal.
☐ 'The carnival was vandalised last night,' Dad said.
☐ Sam flung the bag of sugar into the machine and Ashley flicked the lever to maximum.
☐ A group of carnival workers hurtled towards the elephant seal.
☐ Henry snorted and spat out the tennis ball.
☐ He leaped onto the black rubbery floor of the dodgem rink and threw himself onto the elephant seal.
☐ Henry steamrollered the boat.
☐ 'You think Henry wrecked the carnival stuff, don't you?'

Language usage: of, off

Circle the correct word to complete the following sentences.

Six (of/off) the men worked in the carnival.

He went (of/off) to swim with the elephant seal.

Did you hear the rocket head (of/off)?

Who said you could take the day (of/off)?

(Of/Off) you go to school.

I used to have four (of/off) those balls.

It was one (of/off) his bad days.

He had money so he wasn't too badly (of/off).

Blubber and Floss

Describing words

Write down all the words you can find that the author has used to describe these things or characters.

✴ the teddy bear that Sam won for Max

✴ Henry

✴ the carnival workers

✴ the fairy floss that Ashley squirts at the carnies

Sentence match

Match sentence beginnings to endings

The brown blob splashed and tumbled	an overripe water melon.
Angry shouts came from the carnies	having a mega bad-hair day.
The fisherman snarled and grumbled	into her mouth.
The teddy looked like it was	in the choppy water.
His belly was as round as	who bellowed across the grounds.
The narrow beam of light	as he took off up the beach.
Sam grabbed the hose	lit the path to the beach.
She stuffed a chunk of blue fairy floss	and aimed it at the carnies.

Jimmy and the Bluebottles

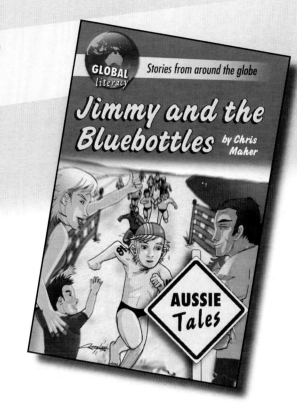

Story facts

Author:	Chris Maher
Illustrator:	Gary Lau
Text Type:	Narrative
Person:	Third
Tense:	Past
Reading level:	26–28

Synopsis

Jimmy is a nipper in the lifesaving club where his father was once club champion. When the coach asks Jimmy to swim in the State Carnival, Jimmy only accepts when he sees the proud look on his father's face. In a practice race, Jimmy is badly stung by bluebottles. The coach saves him but Jimmy no longer wants to be in the competition. On carnival day, Jimmy's younger brother Josh is caught by a strong current. Jimmy overcomes his fear to save him. The race begins and he changes his mind and decides to enter the race as well. The other swimmers are a long way ahead of him but Jimmy swims hard, overtaking most of them. He comes fifth in the race. His father is very proud of him for the brave effort.

Other activities

* As a class, discuss whether there is too much importance placed on being a winner. Encourage the students to give examples that support their opinions.
* In pairs, role-play a telephone conversation between a nipper and a coach. The nipper is trying to find an excuse not to enter the swimming carnival.
* Write a letter to the council giving reasons why they should include nippers in their lifesaving programs.
* You have come first in the County Swimming Carnival and are about to be awarded a trophy. Write a thank-you speech.
* Draw a diagram of a castle. Give it a moat, drawbridge, portcullis, turrets and slit windows. Label these features.
* Locate Wanda and Maroubra Beach on a map of Sydney, and Nambucca Heads on a map of New South Wales.
* Research the history of the lifesaving movement, including nippers.
* Write a paragraph about the appearance, diet, habitat and protective mechanism of a jellyfish.
* List ten other sea creatures dangerous to humans. Circle the one you consider the most dangerous.

Jimmy and the Bluebottles

Grammar

Rewrite the following sentences using correct grammar.

Sometimes if Jimmy done good, his father would buy him a ice-cream.
_____

When is yous gunna have ya race?
_____

Jimmy said he and Josh was going to build a real good sandcastle.
_____

All the Nippers tried to swim quick.
_____

Me and you ain't goin' on the school excursion.
_____

The boy said he never done nothing.
_____

Will you give us a go on your skateboard?
_____

Can you learn me to build a castle outa sand?
_____

Contractions

Combine the following words into one word, using an apostrophe.

could not	_____	I am	_____	you would	_____
you are	_____	we would	_____	we are	_____
can not	_____	they would	_____	they are	_____
were not	_____	she would	_____	I will	_____

Jimmy and the Bluebottles

Glossary

Write the words in the box next to the correct definition.

sprint	tradition	surface	complete
jockey	beach	ice	tentacle
rip	hesitate	avoid	danger
moat	relax	breathe	plaque

custom handed down from one generation to another _____

pause; speak or act with indecision _____

ornamental plate used to record the names of winners _____

thread-like organ used to feel or take hold of things _____

finish an event or task _____

come to the top of a body of water _____

take air into your lungs _____

land along the edge of the sea _____

solid water _____

keep away from someone _____

quick run, short swift foot race _____

risk, menace to safety _____

water-filled trench around a castle _____

swirling, underwater current, dangerous for surfers _____

person who rides racehorses _____

take it easy, unwind, take a break _____

Jimmy and the Bluebottles

Questions

Answer these questions in complete sentences.

What does the expression 'show some bottle' mean?
_____
_____

In what event was Jimmy's mother successful when she was younger?
_____
_____

Describe the effect an onshore wind has on waves.
_____
_____

What three things did Dad say that hurt Jimmy's feelings?
_____
_____

Describe the lifesaving technique Jimmy used to save Josh.
_____
_____

Compound words

Join each word in Column A to a word in Column B to make a compound word.

Column A	Column B	
blue	style	_____
under	stand	_____
life	castle	_____
sand	board	_____
free	saver	_____
surf	bottle	_____

The Crossover

Story facts

Author: Fiona Sievers
Illustrator: Nahum Ziersch & Greg Turra
Text type: Narrative
Person: Third
Tense: Past
Reading level: 30–32

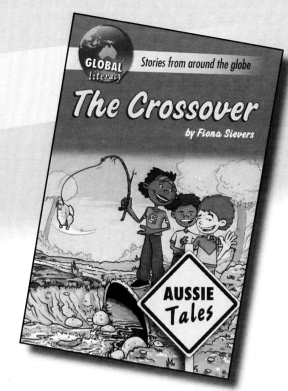

Synopsis

Gemma and Ned hear on the news that cats are disappearing in their town. Their friend Matt calls to tell them that his cat, Boots, is missing as well. The children join forces to search for Boots. They end up in the park at the Crossover, a stream of water. They notice that there is no wildlife around and are curious as to why. As they leave the park, Matt hears a strange noise coming from the water. He is alarmed but tries to convince himself it is nothing. After a night spent worrying about Boots, however, he tells his friends what he heard. The three children return to the Crossover to investigate. They decided to 'fish' for whatever is in the water, using a frozen chicken attached on a rope as bait. The plan works and they discover that there is a crocodile in the stream. They leave the Crossover to consult Gemma and Ned's father, who contacts the police and arranges to meet them at the Crossover. They call in at Matt's house to tell his mother what is happening and Matt is thrilled to find out that Boots has returned safely. Back at the Crossover, the police arrive, along with reptile experts from the zoo and a news team. The zoo officials capture the crocodile and the children are interviewed for a television news story by the reporter.

Other activities

* As a class, discuss whether people should be allowed to kill crocodiles for their skins.

* In pairs, role-play an interview for television about the discovery of the crocodile in the story. One student takes the role of the interviewer, the other takes the role of one of the characters in the story.

* You've lost your pet. Design a 'Missing' poster, describing your pet and where it was last seen.

* Write an information report about the habitat, diet and life cycle of a crocodile.

* Research the differences between freshwater and saltwater crocodiles. Present your findings as a Venn diagram.

* Examine the many different things police do to help people in your community. List as many as you can find.

The Crossover

Proper nouns

Underline the proper nouns in the following sentences.

Ned and Gemma were playing a lively game of snap.

Lots of Australian crocodiles can be found in Queensland.

I don't think there are any crocodiles in the Great Barrier Reef.

Matt called his cat 'Boots'.

Mrs Adams was Gemma and Ned's mother.

Were the reptiles' eggs taken from Taronga Park Zoo?

On Saturday, the children went to look for Matt's cat.

Mr Adams rang Sergeant Collins to tell him about the crocodile.

The children hoped they would be on Channel Seven's news.

'Never Smile at a Crocodile' is the name of a song.

Syllables

Sort the words into the correct column.

Boots	happening	reptile	operation	sedatives	minutes
introduced	crocodile	tonight	scratching	curled	Crossover
television	together	exciting	zoo	disappearing	dangerous

1-syllable word	2-syllable word	3-syllable word	4-syllable word

The Crossover

Word meanings

Write word webs around these topics.

Example:

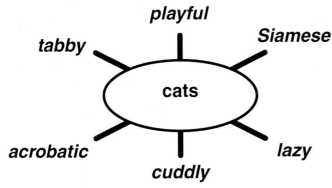

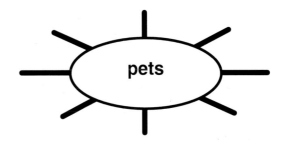

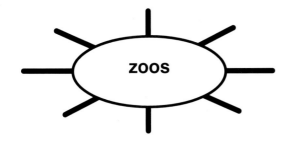

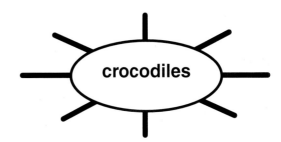

Write the meaning

Use a dictionary to write the meaning of these words.

vegetation _____

breakfast _____

dinosaur _____

garage _____

disappear _____

statue _____

whisper _____

mystery _____

The Crossover

BLM 3

Substituting words

Rewrite the paragraph below, change the underlined words to make it a funny story.

'Could you two please be quiet?' Mrs <u>Adams</u> asked <u>Gemma</u> and <u>Ned</u>. The two children were <u>playing</u> a <u>lively</u> game of <u>Snap</u> in front of the <u>television</u>. Their <u>mother</u> was trying to <u>catch</u> the end of the <u>six</u> o'clock news through their <u>giggles</u> and <u>squeals</u>.

The newsreader said, 'A number of pet cats in <u>Ambrook</u> and surrounding areas have <u>mysteriously</u> <u>disappeared</u>. There are no clues to their whereabouts at this stage. Police are asking <u>anyone</u> with information to come <u>forward</u>.'

_____
_____
_____
_____
_____
_____
_____
_____
_____
_____
_____

Procedure

In *The Crossover*, the children use a frozen chicken as bait to 'fish' for the crocodile. Write a procedure describing the steps for this.

_____
_____
_____
_____
_____
_____

The Copperhead

Story facts

Author:	Delwyne Stephens
Illustrator:	Tom Kurema
Text Type:	Narrative
Person:	Third
Tense:	Past
Reading level:	30–32

Synopsis

One Friday at school, Rachel gets into trouble for accidentally causing another student to hurt herself. Rachel is often in trouble—she finds it difficult to follow her mother's advice to 'stop, think and do the right thing'. After school, Rachel, together with her parents and her younger brother Tim, visits her older brother's farm. Rachel loves being at Roger's farm and loves looking for reptiles. On Saturday morning, Rachel's carelessness leads to a broken fold-up bed and a sore arm for Tim. Rachel's mother is not pleased but Roger comforts her. After breakfast, Rachel, who knows a lot about spiders, insects and reptiles, sets out with Tim to search for a blue-tongue lizard. Against Rachel's wishes, Tim decides to go back to the house because it is too hot. Rachel finds a blue-tongue lizard and at first ignores Tim when he calls out to her. When she does go to him, Rachel finds her brother holding a copperhead snake in his hands. The snake bites Tim. Rachel instructs Tim to lie down and stay perfectly still and runs back to the farm for help. The ambulance is called while Rachel, Dad and Roger run back to Tim. Dad applies a bandage and carries Tim back to the farm. When the ambulance arrives, Rachel is able to clearly tell the ambulance officers what type of snake bit Tim. Tim is taken to hospital, where he recovers. Rachel is considered a hero because of her prompt, sensible behaviour in the face of Tim's accident.

Other activities

* Make a list of Australia's dangerous reptiles, spiders and insects.
* In small groups, debate the topic 'Parents should not make children responsible for their younger brothers and sisters.'
* Brainstorm ways for schools to discipline students other than time-out or detention.
* Compare the old-fashioned treatment for snakebite with the current recommended treatment.
* Choose a reptile and write a short information report on its characteristics.
* Write a cinquain poem entitled 'Snake'.
  Line 1: Subject (noun)—1 word
  Line 2: Description—2 words
  Line 3: Action—3 words
  Line 4: Feeling phrase—4 words
  Line 5: Synonym of title—1 word
* Draw and label the items you'd put in a first aid kit.

The Copperhead

Adjectives

Circle the adjectives in the sentences.

Roger was her older brother.

The children put their schoolbags into the car boot.

They always slept on metal fold-out beds on the back verandah.

These big, black, Australian parrots lived in gum trees.

Tim had forgotten about his sore arm and broken bed.

In it was icy green cordial, two crisp, red apples and chocolate cake.

The large, flat boulder was almost hidden by spiky grass.

Crocodiles, lizards and even friendly looking snakes peeped out from the painted leaves.

Nouns and pronouns

Circle the pronouns, underline the proper nouns and tick the common nouns.

we	Roger	you	their	snake
mother	baby	he	it	us
Rachel	our	spider	lizard	she
your	mine	farm	brother	Tim

The Copperhead

Insects, spiders, reptiles

Read the story to find animals to write under each heading.

Insects	Spiders	Reptiles

Design a book cover

Design an alternative book cover for *Copperhead*, giving it another title and naming yourself as author.

The Copperhead

What, where, who and why

Use complete sentences to answer the following questions.

(See Chapter 1)

What happened to Tamiko after she saw the spider?
_____

What did Rachel have to write out ten times?
_____

What type of animals did Rachel like best?
_____

(See Chapter 2)

Where was Rachel's favourite place in the world?
_____

Where did Dad buy the chips?
_____

At Roger's farm, where did the children sleep?
_____

(See Chapter 3)

Who was woken by the shrill noise of currawongs?
_____

Who had a broken bed and a sore arm?
_____

Who gave Rachel a long, angry look?
_____

(See Chapter 4)

Why did Tim have to hold the blue-tongue lizard properly?
_____

Why did Tim want to go back to the house?
_____

Why did Rachel suggest they have morning tea?
_____

Ratbags

Story facts

Author:	Sandy Fussell
Illustrator:	Peter Viska
Text style:	Narrative
Person	First
Tense:	Past
Reading level:	30–32

Synopsis

Four children belong to the Rescue Agent Team. They call themselves RATs and search the local newspaper hoping to find someone or something to save. They discover that someone has been stealing milk, and a shortage of money is forcing the animal shelter to close. A big reward is offered to anyone who can find the milk-stealing culprit. The RATs accept the challenge and decide to use the reward money, if they're successful, to keep the animal shelter open. The milk mugger turns out to be an old lady who is stealing the milk to feed the animals in the shelter. Rather than tell the police, the children sell her story to the newspaper. The editor chips in money to help as well and the animal shelter remains open.

Other activities

* Find out who Australia's White Mouse was and what she did during the World War II to make her so famous. Present your information in a two-minute speech to the class.

* In small groups, make up a secret club. Write down the name of the club, the aim of the club and three club rules.

* Write a short report about the history of the RSPCA and what it does to care for animals.

* Write a 'letter to the editor', giving your opinion why the local animal shelter should not (or should) be closed down.

* As a class, discuss whether Mrs Johnson stealing the milk was the right thing to do.

Ratbags

Homonyms — by, bye, buy

Write the correct word in the spaces in the sentences.

I told Liam to please _____ a newspaper.

The old granny was _____ herself.

How much will it cost to _____ that house?

A lady at the animal shelter waved good-_____.

A 'no ball' in cricket is called a _____.

Is it your turn to have the _____ at soccer?

Rhyming words

Write a word that rhymes with each of the words below.

team	_____	thing	_____
sounded	_____	whale	_____
growled	_____	groaned	_____
follow	_____	water	_____
world	_____	clean	_____
laying	_____	splatter	_____
sister	_____	money	_____
true	_____	crime	_____
lying	_____	granny	_____

Ratbags
Character description

Describe the physical appearance of the following people.

Liam

_____
_____
_____
_____
_____
_____
_____
_____

Mr Green

_____
_____
_____
_____
_____
_____
_____
_____

Mrs Johnson

_____
_____
_____
_____
_____
_____
_____
_____
_____

May be copied for non-commercial use in purchasing school only.

Ratbags

Word meaning

Without using a dictionary, write a definition of the following words.

judo _____

evil _____

twin _____

reward _____

worry _____

familiar _____

important _____

breakfast _____

Acrostic poem

Write an acrostic poem about the RATs in the story.

R _____

A _____

T _____

B _____

A _____

G _____

S _____

Shape Shifters

Story facts

Author:	Goldie Alexander
Illustrator:	Dion Hamill
Text type:	Narrative
Person:	Third
Tense:	Past
Reading level:	32+

Synopsis

Lei-Lei is a new girl at Penny's school. Acacia, the class bully, tries to steal her lunch. Lei-Lei has special 'shape-shifting' skills and uses them to briefly change Acacia into a prickly tree and stop her bullying. Penny is intrigued and asks Lei-Lei to help her learn to shape-shift. Lei-Lei introduces Penny to her grandmother, Nainai, who teaches Penny the shape-shifting magic. Nainai warns Penny that, while shape-shifting is useful, it can be dangerous when used for the wrong reasons. The girls use their shape-shifting magic on various people and animals, but begin to get careless. Things get out of hand when they decide to change the school principal into a Tasmanian tiger. Penny decides that shape-shifting is too dangerous for her and should be avoided. However, on the way home from school camp, the bus transporting the class blows a tyre and skids into a ditch. Penny decides that this is an occasion where it is right to shape-shift. With the help of Lei-Lei, Penny changes everyone on the bus into soldier ants. The ants use their strong bodies to lift the bus out of the ditch, allowing the driver to change the tyre. Everyone changes back into their human form and arrives home safely.

Other activities

* In small groups, discuss plans of action for when your car breaks down in the country and your mobile phone is out of range.

* How do you think children feel when starting a new school? Write a poem called 'New school'.

* Imagine you could be any animal for 24 hours. Prepare a two-minute speech explaining what animal you would choose and why. Present your speech to the class.

* Imagine that you have a special power. Write a narrative story telling of your adventures.

* List some animals that are either endangered or extinct. Research what scientists are doing to stop animals becoming extinct.

* Investigate what medical science has done to aid patients in need of artificial limbs or organ transplants.

Shape Shifters

Word usage

Prefixes

Choose a prefix from the box to add to the underlined words to give the sentences an opposite meaning.

| im | un | anti | mis | il | in | dis | non | de |

Acacia put her [ ] finished work on the desk.

It rained [ ] frequently while the children were at camp.

Lei-Lei [ ] understood what her grandmother told her.

The teacher told the children to run [ ] clockwise around the circle.

Penny did not always think [ ] logically.

It was [ ] possible for Penny to learn to shape-shift.

The area was classed as [ ] residential.

The magic spell had been [ ] activated.

Nainai [ ] approved of using shape-shifting for fun.

Abbreviations

Write the common abbreviations for the following terms.

television _____

compact disc _____

digital video disc _____

Financial Times _____

North Atlantic Treaty Organisation _____

British Broadcasting Corporation _____

Royal Automobile Club _____

personal identification number _____

master of ceremonies _____

Shape Shifters

True or false

Circle the correct answer.

Lei-Lei's artificial left leg was made out of plastic and metal.	TRUE FALSE
Penny saw her teacher grab Lei-Lei's lunch and throw it away.	TRUE FALSE
Alice was changed into a tree with curly yellow leaves.	TRUE FALSE
Lei-Lei limped because she had an artificial leg.	TRUE FALSE
Penny asked Lei-Lei to teach her to shape-shift.	TRUE FALSE
Bullies are usually very kind and considerate people.	TRUE FALSE
Lei-Lei used her shape-shifting ability to change Delilah into a frog.	TRUE FALSE
A bilby is a harmless Australian marsupial.	TRUE FALSE
A driver almost hit Penny when she was riding her bike.	TRUE FALSE
The word 'solitary' means wanting lots of company.	TRUE FALSE
The girls' teacher couldn't remember being a Tasmanian devil.	TRUE FALSE
'Extinct' means no longer in existence.	TRUE FALSE
The school camp was on the Mornington Peninsula.	TRUE FALSE
The Mornington Peninsula is in Queensland.	TRUE FALSE
Con decided to take a shortcut on the way home from camp.	TRUE FALSE
Lei-Lei and Penny said they wouldn't shape-shift ever again.	TRUE FALSE

Shape Shifters

Punctuation

Rewrite the following with the correct punctuation.

delilah kept on yelling suddenly the wind rose gravel and dust swirled everywhere some flew into pennys eyes when she could see again there was a large black beetle where delilah had been standing the beetle was on its back legs wriggling helplessly

_____
_____
_____
_____
_____
_____

nainai whispered a magic word in pennys ear this is your own special word nainai said to penny never forget it and never tell anyone else penny nodded

_____
_____
_____
_____
_____
_____

Singular and plural words

Change the words from single to plural.

mouse _____	child _____	sheep _____
cry _____	elf _____	eye _____
body _____	glass _____	nose _____
lunch _____	child _____	class _____
bully _____	promise _____	thief _____
box _____	tooth _____	deer _____

May be copied for non-commercial use in purchasing school only.

Macca Dacca

Story facts

Author:	Chris Maher
Illustrator:	Julie Knoblock
Text Type:	Narrative
Person:	Third
Tense:	Past
Reading level:	32+

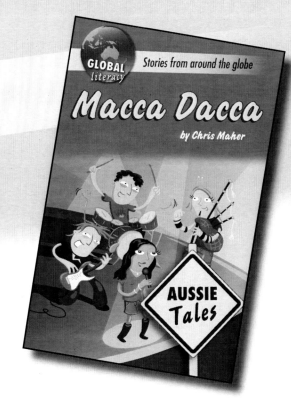

Synopsis

Angus and Ahmed are best friends. They love rock and roll music. Angus plays the guitar and Ahmed practises playing the drums on pots and pans. They call themselves Macca Dacca and dream of playing in a famous band one day. When their teacher tells them about a band competition, the boys decide to enter. They convince Angus's sister to play the bagpipes and they also recruit Mele, a gospel singer, to be their lead vocalist. On the day of the concert, nobody wants to listen to Macca Dacca until Mele decides to sing one of her gospel songs. The rest of the band accompany her and they win the competition.

Other activities

✴ Do you think pop stars deserve the huge amount of money they earn? Discuss in small groups.

✴ What's your favourite band and why do you like them?

✴ Role-play a phone call to a famous pop star inviting him or her to perform at your school.

✴ Design a poster to advertise a school concert.

✴ Imagine that Angus has grown up and become famous. You are the president of his fan club. Write a letter to Angus telling him how much you enjoy his music.

✴ Choose one of these instruments: guitar, drums or bagpipes. Write a report about how they're made, where they originated and how they're played.

Macca Dacca

Proofreading

Underline the mistakes in the following sentences, then rewrite each sentence correctly.

Angus said 'Youse two aren't going to win no competition.'

_____

Me and Ahmed are going to win the prize.

_____

I wonder what I done with my Guitar.

_____

the kids from up the road is coming to the concert with you.

_____

Was Drews guitar a Stratocaster.

_____

All the bands is very nervous.

_____

Mark skinners' group was called masculine.

_____

The crowd shouted and clap because they likes the song.

_____

Punctuation

Put the apostrophe in the correct place in the underlined words. There might be more than one correct place in some sentences.

It was <u>Mels</u> voice they heard.

The <u>boxes</u> labels were coming off.

She put the equipment in her <u>fathers</u> car.

The two <u>girls</u> screams were deafening.

It was a battle to win the final <u>competitions</u> prize.

Those <u>churches</u> music is nearly always gospel.

This <u>evenings</u> newspaper was late.

Macca Dacca

Why? Because!

Match the beginning of each sentence to its correct ending.

Mr Leadbelly reached into his drawer

Angus thought Mark was stupid to wear aftershave

Ahmed played drums on the pots and pans

The boys called the band Macca Dacca

Angus wanted Mele to join the band

Drew didn't have a lot of time to practise

Mark said his band was called Masculine

Angus could hardly walk before his item

They called the new band ADAM

because she had to study.

because he wasn't old enough to shave.

because they were all boys.

because he was so nervous.

because it stood for the initials of the bandmembers' first names.

because he wanted to get some paper.

because he didn't have a drum kit.

because it was a combination of AC/DC and Ahmed's nickname.

because she had a lovely singing voice.

Write a different ending

Oh no! The band has lost the competition. Write some sentences to give the story a different ending.

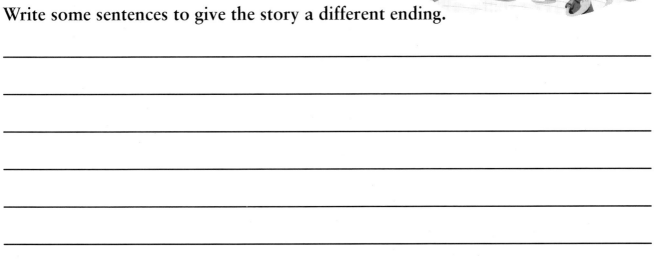

_____
_____
_____
_____
_____
_____

Macca Dacca

Crossword fun

Across

2 Battle of the _____

5 Mele sang in a church _____

7 Skinner's first name

8 The instrument Drew played in Macca Dacca

Down

1 What type of instrument is a Stratocaster?

3 The instrument that Ahmed played

4 Angus' favourite band

6 The name of Angus' sister